SERIES EDITOR: LEE J

OSPREY NEW VANGUARD

PANZERKAMPFWAGEN III
MEDIUM TANK
1936–1944

TEXT BY
BRYAN PERRETT

COLOUR ARTWORK BY
DAVID E. SMITH, MIKE CHAPPELL and MIKE BADROCKE

OSPREY
MILITARY

First published in Great Britain in 1999 by Osprey Publishing,
Elms Court, Chapel Way, Botley, Oxford OX2 9LP, UK

ISBN 1 85532 845 3

Editor: Marcus Cowper
Design: Daniel Aspery
Colour plates by David E. Smith and Mike Chappell
Cutaway artwork by Mike Badrocke
Cutaway annotation by Hilary Doyle

Origination by Valhaven Ltd, Isleworth, UK
Printed through World Print Ltd, Hong Kong

98 99 00 01 02   10 9 8 7 6 5 4 3 2 1

FOR A CATALOGUE OF ALL BOOKS PUBLISHED BY OSPREY MILITARY,
AUTOMOTIVE AND AVIATION, PLEASE WRITE TO:
The Marketing Manager
Osprey Publishing, PO Box 140, Wellingborough, Northants,
NN8 4ZA, United Kingdom

OR VISIT THE OSPREY WEBSITE AT:
http:/www.osprey-publishing.co.uk

Publisher's note

Readers may wish to study this title in conjunction with the
following Osprey publications:

New Vanguard 1 *Kingtiger – Heavy Tank – 1942–45*
New Vanguard 5 *Tiger 1 – Heavy Tank – 1942–45*
New Vanguard 15 *Flammpanzer – German Flamethrowers 1941–45*
New Vanguard 19 *Stug III – Assault Gun 1940–45*
New Vanguard 22 *Panther Variants 1942–45*
New Vanguard 25 *SdKfz 251 Half-Track 1939–45*
New Vanguard 26 *German Light Panzers 1932–42*
MAA 24 *Panzer Divisions*
Campaign 5 *Ardennes 1944*
Campaign 16 *Kursk 1943*
Campaign 42 *Operation Bagration 1944*

Editor's note

The Editor would like to express his thanks to David Fletcher, the
Curator of the RAC Tank Museum, Bovington, for his help in the
preparation of this title.
This book is a revised edition of Vanguard 16
The Panzerkampwagen III, first published in 1980. The text has
been revised, new black and white photos included and a detailed
cutaway of a PzKpfw III added.

Artist's note

Readers may care to note that the original artwork from which the
cutaway plate in this book was prepared is available for private sale.
All reproduction copyright whatsoever is retained by the publisher.
All enquiries should be addressed to:

Mike Badrocke, 37 Prospect Road, Southborough, Tunbridge Wells,
Kent TN4 0EN UK

The publishers regret that they can enter into no correspondence on
this matter.

TITLE PAGE **PzKpfw III Ausf. J in winter whitewash colour
scheme, Russia, 1942–1943. To protect their moving parts
from the arctic conditions, the co-axial and hull machine-
guns have been covered with canvas sleeves. A small pile
of kindling can be seen drying out on the engine deck.
(Charles K. Kliment)**

PANZERKAMPFWAGEN III MEDIUM TANK 1936–1944

DEVELOPMENT

On 16 March 1935 the German government formally repudiated the disarmament clauses of the Treaty of Versailles, which contained the strict proviso that Germany was prohibited from owning or obtaining tracked armoured fighting vehicles. Hitler had calculated correctly that British and French reaction to the repudiation would be limited to toothless bluster, and having thus presented the world with a *fait accompli*, set about building up his armed services by the introduction of universal conscription and the initiation of a vast arms production programme.

Although herself forbidden to manufacture tanks while the Treaty provisions applied, Germany was far from being totally lacking in tank design experience. In the years following the Great War, she had co-operated with that other contemporary international pariah, Bolshevik Russia, in establishing a secret experimental station on the Karma River, although the result of the joint research programme tended to be of greater benefit to the Red Army; Sweden had also provided some practical assistance.

In addition to the experimental prototypes constructed in conjunction with the Russians, two light tanks had been designed and were actually in process of manufacture under the guise of agricultural tractors when the repudiation took place. These became known as the PzKpfw I and PzKpfw II, their intended rôles being

PzKpfw III Ausf. A photographed in Poland, 1939. The Ausf. A – D were fitted with a circular hull machine gun mounting. Note yellow turret cross; see Plate A1 and commentary. (Bundesarchiv)

respectively training and reconnaissance. As these vehicles left the production lines they were sent immediately to the newly formed Panzer divisions as temporary expedients pending the appearance of purpose-built main battle tanks, the plan being that each battalion should consist of one Heavy Company, equipped with tanks carrying a large-calibre gun for close support, and three Medium Companies, whose tanks would carry an armour-defeating gun and two machine guns. In due course the mount of the Heavy Company would become known as the PzKpfw IV, and that of the Medium Companies as the PzKpfw III.

The starting point for the PzKpfw III design, as in every main battle tank design, was the gun. Senior tank officers requested a 50mm gun; a sensible provision at a time when the British were beginning to fit a 40mm 2pdr. gun into their new Cruiser tanks, and the Russians were already employing a 45mm gun in their BTs and T-26s. However, the **Heereswaffenamt**, responsible for procurement, demurred, pointing out with the backing of the Artillery Inspectorate that the infantry was already in possession of the 37mm anti-tank gun, which was in quantity production, and the obvious desirability of standardisation of armour-piercing ammunition and weapons. An intelligent compromise was reached by which the tank officers accepted the 37mm, while the turret ring was to be constructed wide enough to accommodate the 50mm gun if necessary.

Having settled this question, the next step was to design the hull within the then 24-ton German bridge-loading specification (Contemporary British designers were similarly hampered by a mandatory railway loading gauge restriction. This had the effect of limiting the width of their tanks, and thus the turret ring, and so

An early Ausf. E of 3.Panzer-regiment, 2.Panzer-Division en route for Greece during the 1941 Balkan campaign. Other photographs of this unit confirm the distinctive style of markings, with a small white vehicle number on the hull side well forward, tactical symbols on the turret side, and a horse-shoe displayed on the track-guard. See Plate A2 and commentary. (Bundesarchiv)

ultimately the size of the weapon that could be mounted). A standard layout was adopted with the engine mounted at the rear. Inside the turret the commander sat centrally beneath his cupola, with the gunner on the left of the gun breech and the loader on the right. In the forward compartment the driver was located on the left and the radio operator/hull gunner on the right, with the transmission between them. The final drive ran to the sprockets across the front of the forward compartment. This basic arrangement remained unaltered throughout the vehicle's history.

Once the prototypes had been produced and tested, Daimler-Benz were appointed to oversee development and manufacture, the essential requirements being specified as a 15-ton vehicle capable of 25mph. The true purpose of the vehicle was cloaked under the security title of **Zugführerwagen** or ZW ('platoon commander's vehicle'); but military bureaucracy being as self-perpetuating as any other kind, successive Marks carried in addition to their Ausführung letter a progressive ZW number, long after security had ceased to be an overriding consideration.

The **Ausführung A** appeared in 1936. The running gear consisted of five medium-sized roadwheels, front drive sprocket, spoked idler and two return rollers. The vehicle was powered by a 250hp 12-cylinder Maybach 108TR engine, and transmission was by means of a five-speed gearbox, which also provided one reverse gear. The L/45 37mm main armament

**Ausf. M, knocked out in Tunisia. The progressive up-gunning and up-armouring of the PzKpfw III are very striking if one compares this to the previous picture: note L/60 gun, spaced armour mantlet, and appliqué armour bolted across the front plate. From the Ausf. J onwards the hull machine gun mounting reverted to the round type. The turret number '6', in black, trimmed with either red or yellow, probably refers to the company – this was normal practice with single-digit presentations.
(RAC Tank Museum)**

was mounted co-axially with twin 7.92mm machine guns behind a recessed mantlet which was vulnerable to bullet splash, while a further 7.92mm machine gun was carried in a ball mounting in the front plate of the hull. The commander's cupola was starkly simple, consisting of a slotted 'dustbin', and the turret was fitted with one-piece side hatches.

Daimler-Benz had hit their weight target by providing a maximum armour thickness of 14.5mm, but the suspension system was more suitable for commercial than military usage and the engine output was comparatively low, so that the vehicle's top speed of 20mph fell below the required specification. Ten vehicles of this type were produced.

The **Ausführung B** was broadly similar in its concept, but attempted to solve the suspension problem by employing leaf instead of coil springs, eight smaller road wheels being suspended from two horizontal spring units, while the number of return rollers was increased to three. This had the effect of raising the weight slightly to 15.9 tons, but achieved a modest increase in speed of 1.7mph. The chassis is of some interest in that it provided the basis for the prototype Sturmgeschütz (see New Vanguard 19 *StuG III Assault Gun 1940–1942*).

Ausführung C was almost identical but provided an alternative method of leaf-spring arrangement, employing one large central unit and two smaller units fore and aft. Ausf. B and C were produced concurrently in 1937, 15 vehicles of each type being built.

Ostensibly **Ausführung D**, which appeared late in 1938 was a further variation on the eightwheel leaf-spring suspension theme, in which the fore and aft units carried by the Ausf. C were angled slightly inwards. However, maximum armour thickness had been increased to 30mm and a more workmanlike cupola introduced, which was not only lower but which also provided latched visors for the protection of the vision blocks. These improvements raised the vehicle's weight to 19 tons, but the installation of a better gearbox containing an additional forward gear maintained the maximum speed obtainable on previous models. Some 29 vehicles of this type were built, and the earlier Marks were also up-armoured to the 30mm standard. Ausf. A to D all carried 120 rounds of main and 4,425 rounds of secondary armament ammunition.

1939 saw the appearance of the **Ausführung E**, which finally

PzKpfw III fording the river Drut, USSR, July 1941. The vehicle has been identified as belonging to 9.Panzer-Division. (US National Archives)

Loader's view of main and co-axial armament. The muzzle-heavy 50mm L/42 gun is indicated by the counterweight ingot just discernible in the back of the spent case deflector shield, so this is presumably either an Ausf. H or early J, or an up-gunned F or G. (Imperial War Museum)

overcame the difficulties which had been experienced with the suspension. A robust torsion bar system was adopted, emptying six small road wheels. The redesign of the running gear also incorporated a new disc idler, and the position of the three return rollers was slightly altered.

This Mark was driven by the 300hp 12-cylinder Maybach HL I20TR engine, and the manual gearbox employed on the earlier models was replaced by the Maybach Variorex pre-selector box which provided 10 forward and one reverse gears. Although the vehicle's weight was now 20 tons the more powerful engine produced a top speed of 25mph.

Changes in the turret design included the introduction of two-piece side hatches. Early examples of the production run show the retention of the twin co-axial machine guns and an internal mantlet, but as the series progressed the co-axial armament was reduced to one gun and an external mantlet was adopted. Hull escape hatches for the driver and radio operator were installed above the second and third road wheels although, again, these do not appear on the early versions. Estimates of production figures for the Ausf. E vary considerably, the most likely figure being in the region of one hundred.

The **Ausführung F** also began production in 1939, the early vehicles being almost indistinguishable from the first Ausf. Es, mounting a 37mm gun and twin machine guns behind an internal mantlet. However, on this model new ventilation ducts for the track brakes had been installed, and the covers for these were visible on the glacis plate.

By now the wisdom of the original proposal to fit a 50mm main armament had become apparent, and later vehicles in the series were fitted with the L/42 50mm gun in conjunction with a single co-axial machine gun, the mounting being protected by an external mantlet. This gun was also fitted retrospectively to the Ausf. E.

Ausführung G, which first appeared in October 1940, presented little external difference from its immediate predecessor, but possessed an improved commander's cupola. The first few vehicles mounted the 37mm main armament, but thereafter the L/42 50mm gun was fitted as standard. The Ausf. G was modified for service in North Africa by the provision of larger radiators and an additional air filter made from felt.

Experience in Poland and France had indicated that the PzKpfw III was under-armoured. A temporary method of correcting this would have been to add external plating to the vulnerable areas, but the suspension was already considered to be carrying its maximum load and a further increase in ground pressure was not thought to be desirable. It was therefore necessary to redesign the basic running gear to allow for the additional weight, and this resulted in the **Ausführung H**.

On this model the torsion bar suspension was strengthened and the track width increased from 36cm to 40cm. To compensate for this, new sprockets and idlers were introduced, the former having six apertures as opposed to eight circular holes, and the latter being of an eight-spoked type. Existing stocks of the old sprockets and idlers were also used in conjunction with spacer rings. The opportunity was also taken to replace the complicated Variorex pre-selector gearbox with the simpler Aphon synchromesh, which provided six forward and one reverse gears. Additional 30mm plates were fixed to the bow, driver's and stern plates, but although this increased the vehicle's weight to 21.6 tons the ground pressure actually showed a slight decrease, and the maximum speed remained unaltered.

The Ausf. H began entering service at the end of 1940 and was fitted with the L/42 50mm gun, for which a total of 99 rounds could be stowed, together with 3,750 rounds for the secondary armament. Like the Ausf. F and G it carried a rack of smoke bombs in a prominent box at the rear, the operation of which is described below.

The addition of appliqué armour could, however, only be regarded as a temporary expedient pending the production of a basic up-armoured design. This appeared in 1941 as the **Ausführung J**, which carried integral 50mm front and rear armour. An internal improvement was the provision of levers in place of the pedals which had activated the steering brakes on previous models.

Following the fall of France, Hitler, with considerable prescience, had given orders that the PzKpfw III's main armament should be the longer L/60 50mm gun. Partly because of supply difficulties, these instructions had been ignored, so that when faced with the 76.2mm weapons of the T-34 and KV-I in Russia the vehicle was caught badly short. Furious at this disobedience, the Führer flew into one of his rages, unfairly describing the PzKpfw III as an unsuccessful design. After the first Ausf. Js had been produced with the L/42 gun, the L/60 weapon was fitted as standard, and earlier models which were returned to Germany for refit were also up-gunned. Stowage of main armament ammunition for the L/60 gun was limited to 78 rounds.

Balancing the L/60 gun of the later Ausf. J posed a more serious problem, which was sometimes solved by a compression spring mounted in a cylinder and attached to the gun. This can be seen on the right of the picture, and in the foreground to the right of it is the supplementary traverse handle fitted to some vehicles; this enabled the loader to assist the gunner, to whose controls it was linked under the gun. (Imperial War Museum)

The 'sight picture' of a PzKpfw III with 50mm gun: (1) Range plate (2) Sighting plate (3) Main armament engaging hard target at l,000m (4) Co-axial MG engaging infantry at 400m.

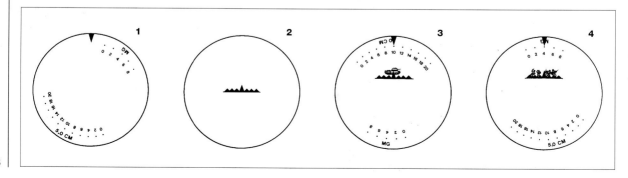

Gunner's view of the turret of an L/60-armed Ausf. J. Note commander's voice-tube, and immediately below it a case for spare MG barrels stowed on the turret ring. (Martin Windrow)

Looking forward from the loader's position in the same turret; note details of co-axial MG mounting. (Martin Windrow)

The Ausf. J began reaching regiments at the end of 1941, by which time it was already apparent that a 50mm armour base was inadequate. In order to minimise the weight increase inevitable with the addition of further appliqué armour, it was decided to employ a spaced armour system, 20mm plates being mounted slightly ahead of the front plate and mantlet. This, together with the larger main armament, increased the tank's weight to 22.3 tons. In this version the vehicle was known as the **Ausführung L**.

The **Ausführung M** appeared in 1942 and closely resembled the Ausf. L. It was, however, fitted with a self-sealing exhaust system which enabled it to wade unprepared to a depth of five feet, this being located at the extreme rear of the vehicle. Two batteries of three smoke-bomb dischargers were fitted to the turret sides, arranged so as to drop a pattern ahead of the tank if fired simultaneously.

Between the end of 1941 and the spring of 1943 a total of 1,969 L/60 50mm PzKpfw IIIs were built, but it had long been apparent that the design could not absorb further attempts at up-gunning and up-armouring. The rôle of the German Army's main battle tank had passed to the PzKpfw IV; the final version of the PzKpfw III, the **Ausführung N**, mounted an L/24 howitzer inherited from the early models of the PzKpfw IV which had once equipped the Heavy Companies of the standard tank battalions. Stowing 64 rounds, these vehicles, of which some 660 were built, were employed in the fire-support rôle with Panzergrenadier Divisions and the newly-formed Heavy Tank Battalions; in the latter case, they lingered on in battalion and company headquarters long after Tigers began reaching their units regularly.

Production of the PzKpfw III ended in August 1943, although the chassis continued to be used in the construction of assault guns. Latterly, the development of hollow charge munitions, capable of being fired at comparatively close quarters by infantry from a hand held projector, meant that the main armour had to be shielded by 5mm side skirts and turret girdles, so permitting the worst effects of the explosion to disperse in the space between. At about the same time, a coating of *Zimmerit* anti-magnetic mine paste was applied.

SPECIAL-PURPOSE VEHICLES

An interesting variation was the **Tauchpanzer** ('diving tank'), which was designed in 1940 for the invasion of Great Britain. All openings to the exterior of the vehicle were sealed with a watertight compound and the gap between hull and turret closed by an inflatable rubber ring. Rubber sheeting covered the commander's cupola, the mantlet and the hull machine gun, but this could be blown away from inside the vehicle by means of an electrical detonator. Air was supplied to the engine by a flexible 18-metre hose which was held on the surface by a buoy, while exhaust gases were carried upwards through two tall vertical pipes fitted with non-return valves. Maximum safe diving depth was 15 metres, and the crew's submerged endurance set at 20 minutes.

The intention was for the tanks to launch themselves from lighters and then motor ashore along the seabed, direction being maintained by instructions passed through a radio link from the parent vessel. The design was, on the whole, successful and found a practical application at the crossing of the River Bug during Operation 'Barbarossa'. The crews were drawn from volunteer battalions, which were later formed into the 18th Panzer Regiment.

The Ausf. M formed the basis of a flame-throwing tank; the official designation of which was **PzKpfw III (Flam)**. The flame projector tube replaced the conventional 50mm gun in the mantlet, and was recognisable by being somewhat thicker. One hundred litres of flame liquid were stored inboard and driven through the projector tube by a two-stroke engine. By restricting bursts to two or three seconds' duration it was possible to obtain up to 80 flame-shots with a maximum range of 60 yards. The crew consisted of a commander/flame gunner, radio operator/hull gunner and driver. One hundred of these conversions were made, serving in specialist battalions 20 to 30 strong, and employed at the discretion of senior commanders.

The *Tauchpanzer,* or Diving Tank, seen here during trials for Operation 'Sea Lion'. Vehicles of this type were used successfully in the crossing of the River Bug during the initial stages of 'Barbarossa' in June 1941. (Bundesarchiv)

A Panzerbefehlswagen III of 15.Panzer-Division, whose sign appears in red on the front trackguard. The marking of the national cross on the hull front was most unusual. (RAC Tank Museum)

A slightly offbeat development was the fitting of an Ausf. N onto a railway mounting to which the line of drive was passed by means of spindles. The vehicle was intended to patrol railways in Russia and keep them free from partisan interference, but the idea offered little that an armoured train did not, was extremely expensive, and did not proceed beyond the prototype phase.

The PzKpfw III was widely used for conversion to the role of **Panzer-befehlswagen** ('armoured command vehicle'). Versions were produced on the Ausf. D, E and H chassis, and all followed the same pattern with a fixed turret (usually bolted to the hull) mounting a dummy gun, and an unmistakable 'bedstead' loop aerial over the engine deck.

A report by the School of Tank Technology on a captured example based on an Ausf. H chassis notes that the turret roof was reinforced by an extra 15mm plate, presumably as a defence against mortar fire. The mantlet was moulded in light alloy and modelled on that of the Ausf. D. Radio equipment consisted of two sets mounted at the rear of the command compartment, directly above the propeller shaft and connected to the loop aerial. Two further sets were fitted to the forward hull wall, and a further two above the gearbox. Additional vision ports had been provided, and the report also noted the provision of cushioned seats and backrests of a more 'luxurious standard' than those employed in gun tanks, but the term is entirely relative.

The captured example did not contain a map table, but this would normally have been a standard fitting. Originally the Panzerbefehlswagen III was classed as a large command vehicle for use by regimental commanders and above, and there is good reason to believe that vehicles used by certain higher formation commanders contained the Enigma portable trans-coding device. Later in the war, as more vehicles became available, large ACVs were issued to battalion commanders.

The flame-thrower version of the PzKpfw III closely resembled the Ausf. L and M, but was recognisable by the thicker barrel of the flame projector tube. The cylinder dimly visible at hull rear is part of the deep-wading exhaust system. (Imperial War Museum)

One problem with the Panzerbefehlswagen was the easy identification provided by its distinctive loop aerial, which was replaced in 1943 by more conventional rods. Again, command vehicles were just as subject to breakdown as any other and their loss at a critical moment could have serious consequences. To provide immediate first-line replacement, regiments were from the autumn of 1942 issued with a basic PzKpfw III gun tank with additional radio facilities, this being known as the Panzerbefehlswagen III Ausf. K.

Until 1943 Panzerartillerie Forward Observation Officers performed their duties from a light half-track which, because of its vulnerability, was not entirely suitable for the task. However, in that year numbers of PzKpfw III gun tanks were specially converted for the role, their title being **Panzerbeobachtungswagen** ('armoured observation vehicle') **III**. In this version the main armament was stripped out and replaced by a single ball-mounted machine gun in the centre of the mantlet, a dummy gun being installed to its right. The interior contained an artillery board and duplicate radios, one netted to the main operational frequency, the other providing a rear link to the guns. The crew consisted of the FOO, his technical assistant, two radio operators and the driver, all of whom would have been artillery personnel.

The PzKpfw III's most enduring offspring was, without doubt, the Sturmgeschütz (StuG) or assault gun. This consisted of the standard PzKpfw III chassis on which a low, fixed superstructure was built well forward, mounting first the L/24 75mm howitzer carried by early models of the PzKpfw IV and, later, the L/43 or L/48 75mm high-velocity guns or a 105mm howitzer. The StuG formed the principal equipment of the Sturmartillerie, an élite branch of the artillery dedicated to close infantry support, which considered itself to be every inch the equal of the Panzertruppen. A total of 10,500 StuGs were built on the PzKpfw chassis, mainly by Alkett of Berlin, accounting for more than three times their number of enemy fighting vehicles. Latterly, as a result of the general shortage of equipment, panzer regiments were glad to supplement their few remaining tanks with assault guns, so in that form at least the PzKpfw III can be said to have served throughout the war. The history, development and tactical employment of the assault gun is more fully discussed in New Vanguard 19 *StuG III Assault Gun 1940-42*.

In 1942 fighting within the built-up areas of Stalingrad indicated that a heavier weapon was needed than the 75mm howitzer carried by the assault gun. First choice fell on the 150mm Infantry Gun 33, which at that time was fitted to the chassis of the PzKpfw I, PzKpfw II and 38T, some of which were grossly overloaded; moreover, the open-topped superstructures of these vehicles made them unsuitable for street-fighting.

In an attempt to overcome these difficulties, the chassis of the PzKpfw III was used as the basis for an experimental vehicle known as the **Sturm-Infanteriegeschütz 33**. Layout followed that of the assault gun, the weapon being mounted in a fixed enclosed superstructure with 80mm frontal armour. The vehicle weighed 22 tons, was manned by a crew of five, and had a maximum speed of 12mph; 30 rounds of main armament ammunition were carried. In the event the design was overtaken by the heavy assault gun Brummbär, which was based on the PzKpfw IV chassis. Production of the Sturm-Infanteriegeschütz 33 terminated in November 1942, by which time only 24 vehicles had been produced. They are reported as having equipped the 9th Company of Panzer Regiment 201 during the summer of 1943.

Other PzKpfw III variants included a very simple recovery vehicle, the **Bergepanzerwagen III**, which consisted of a turretless hull, fitted with towing attachments; and a supply carrier, the **Schlepper III**, which carried a large wooden box superstructure in place of the turret. Turretless versions also carried ammunition in the forward zone, and the heavy equipment required by the Panzer divisions' assault engineer units. Experiments were carried out with a prototype mine-clearing vehicle, which achieved extra ground clearance by means of extension arms, but very few details are available.

By September 1941 PzKpfw III and PzKpfw IV were performing a similar battlefield rôle, and as the two designs had much in common it was felt that numerous benefits, including standardisation of parts, would accrue if they were to be merged. The composite vehicle was given the title of **PzKpfw III/IV**, and several prototypes were constructed in which the parentage of the hull and turret was clearly identifiable, although the suspension now carried six large interleaved wheels. The design was ingenious but became a casualty in the accelerating gun/armour race, and was finally abandoned in 1944.

The German Army relied on verbal orders to a greater extent than other armies, thus accelerating the command process considerably. Here two *Panzerbefehlswagen* III have met for an orders group in Russia; while senior officers confer with maps, lesser mortals such as drivers remove themselves to a respectful distance. (Bundesarchiv)

PZKPFW III DESCRIBED

Armour

In April 1943 Messrs William Beardmore & Co. Ltd. of Glasgow analysed several samples of the armour plate used to construct the PzKpfw III, the consultants drawing the following conclusions:

'All the material has been made in the electric furnace and the compositions vary considerably, possibly because of different sources of supply. In every case the Carbon content is higher than is used here, whilst the combination of high Silicon and high Chromium is rather an unusual feature. The physical properties approximate to our own bullet-proof material but as a whole it does not show any improvement over this. With regard to the welding which is present at various points, this is extremely poor in all cases.'

These comments were amplified by the Ministry of Supply following detailed examination of the hull and turret of a captured Ausf. J:

'The problem of making a battle-worthy structure in this comparatively high carbon armour, using hard-surfacing and austenitic electrodes and at the same time giving assistance to the welds by means of riveted plate edges, *was not overcome*. The extent of cracking suggests that pre-heating was not adopted. Judged by any standards, the behaviour of the welding is unsatisfactory.'

Automotive

The Maybach engine had been designed to operate in temperate climates, in which it performed satisfactorily. However, in tropical or dusty conditions it was subject to breakdown and overheating, and a British intelligence summary dated 18 February 1942, prepared after examination of abandoned vehicles, commented on the number of failures due to engine and bogie problems.

'The engine trouble was due chiefly to sand blocking oil supply pipes damaging crankshafts and pistons, and sand in the distributor, dynamo and starter. The air filter is entirely inadequate. Bogie trouble was due to the disintegration of tyres due to high speed or heat.'

The user handbook recommended a maximum engine speed of 2,600rpm for normal usage, but in hot climates, which included southern Russia as well as North Africa, it was suggested that employment of a lower gear than was necessary would produce cooler running. Use of the engine as a brake was permissible at 2,200-2,400rpm, but was to be avoided in the 2,600-3,300rpm band. Overheated engines tended to 'diesel' after being switched off, a fault which could be corrected by switching on again and either opening the throttle or idling until the temperature dropped. The principal components in the cooling system were two radiators with a total effective area of 5½ square feet, through which air was dragged by two fans.

The Variorex pre-selector gearbox was considered to be effective up to seventh gear, after which the tractive effort fell away sharply. The eighth gear was suitable for level road running, but the ninth and tenth gears were regarded as

The armoured artillery observation vehicle, *Panzerbeobachtungswagen III*, was easily recognisable by its off-centre dummy gun; effective armament was limited to a single ball-mounted machine gun in the centre of the mantlet. (Imperial War Museum)

The *Bergepanzerwagen III* was a simple turretless towing vehicle; foul-weather protection was provided by a collapsible canvas hood, propped open in this Russian winter scene. (Bundesarchiv)

overdrives and seldom used. The Aphon synchromesh gearbox drew favourable comment, although once again the tractive effort in top (i.e. sixth) gear was low, and this was largely reserved for road use. For both systems it was recommended that 'when changing to a lower gear on turnings, hills or bad roads, *two* gears lower than the one already engaged should be selected.'

The final drive and steering brake assembly was extremely complicated. An excessive number of ball races were incorporated and, as already mentioned, considerable care was taken to provide an air cooling system for the track brake drums. Even so, there was no automatic equalisation of the torque on the two output shafts, and the mechanism did not provide positive steering when both steering brakes were released.

The torsion bar suspension was adequate, although in sandy areas grit tended to penetrate the shock absorbers, shortening their life. Track tension was achieved by means of a bell crank. On the Eastern Front track extensions known as *Ostketten* were fitted to increase traction during the winter months, usually to one track only – a most dangerous practice in any sort of hilly country.

An electric self-starter was provided, but this was for use in emergency only, and never with a cold engine. The normal method of starting was by means of an inertia system, the starting handle entering the engine compartment through the tail plate. The handle was swung by two men until the flywheel had reached 60rpm, when the power was tripped to turn the main engine. The inertia starter was geared, but its operation in the depths of the Russian winter, with sump oil chilled to the consistency of treacle, required a great deal of initial effort, although the driver could eliminate the additional drag of the gear-box oil by depressing his clutch. Cold starting was assisted by a starter carburettor which was not to be used in conjunction with the accelerator. Minimum unassisted working temperature for the engine was 50 degrees centigrade at 2,000rpm with an oil pressure of not less than 60lb per square inch.

Gunnery and Optical

Elevation of the main and co-axial armament was by means of a handwheel operated with the gunner's left hand. Immediately to the right of this was the traversing handwheel, which included a release latch and which was sometimes linked under the gun to a hand crank which could be turned by the loader. The traverse mechanism incorporated two gears, one requiring 88 turns of the handwheel to achieve a complete revolution of the turret, and the other, used for fine laying, 132 turns. The main armament was fired electrically and its recoil was controlled by a hydro-pneumatic buffer system containing a filling liquid which was simply known as Braun.

The 50mm guns carried by the PzKpfw III were muzzle heavy in their mounting. In the case of the L/42 model, this was easily corrected by the addition of a lead weight to the rear of the spent case deflector shield. However, the imbalance became even more pronounced when the longer L/60 model was fitted, and to compensate for this a small compression spring in a cylinder was mounted on the forward offside corner of the turret ring and attached to the gun. This arrangement was found on the Ausf. J, but on later Marks a torsion bar was bolted across the turret roof and connected to the upper part of the gun mounting. On later Marks, too, the recoil shield arms were 4½in. longer, providing additional compensation but reducing clearance to the turret ring to 17½in.

The sighting telescope was more complicated than its British counterpart, which employed a simple graticule pattern, and contained two movable plates. The first or range plate rotated about its own axis, the main armament and machine gun scales being marked on opposing quadrants; the 50mm scale was marked from 0 to 2,000 metres, and the machine gun scale from 0 to 800 metres. The second or sighting plate moved in a vertical plane and contained the sighting and aim-off markings. The two plates moved simultaneously, the sighting plate rising or falling as the range plate turned. To engage at a selected range, the range wheel was turned until the required marking was opposite the pointer at the top of the sight, and the sighting mark laid onto the target by the traverse and elevation controls.

Ammunition stowage in vehicles fitted with the L/42 50mm gun was as follows:

Under the gunner's seat: 5 rounds
In locker situated at right/rear of fighting compartment: 22 rounds
In locker immediately above: 12 rounds
In locker situated at left/rear compartment: 36 rounds
In locker immediately above: 24 rounds
Total: 99 rounds.

A well-camouflaged *Panzerbeobachtungswagen III* (armoured observation vehicle), used by the Panzer division's artillery forward observation officers to control the fire of their guns. The vehicle is identified by its dummy gun offset to the right. Armament consisted of a ball-mounted machine gun in the centre of the mantlet. (RAC Tank Museum)

The Panzer III fared very badly in its first encounters with the British Matilda. Prodigious efforts to increase their protection with bogies and track links did not save this crew, apparently. (Imperial War Museum)

With the exception of the rounds under the gunner's seat, all ammunition was stowed vertically, the case fitting into a recess in the locker floor while the nose was held in place by a spring clip. The arrangement was neat, but made withdrawal of certain rounds difficult. The right lower locker and two left/rear lockers were closed by sliding doors, which tended to jam with sand particles; the right upper locker was fitted with a hinged door. On L/60 50mm vehicles a horizontal stowage pattern was adopted for ready-use rounds.

Whatever system was employed, the loader laboured under something of a disadvantage in that the turret floor was fixed and he was forced to 'walk after' the gun breech whenever the turret was traversed. The commander and gunner were more fortunate in that their seats were attached to the turret itself.

Machine gun ammunition was distributed along the walls of the fighting and hull gunner's compartments in bags, each bag containing a 150-round belt. The bag system was less efficient than the British metal box 'liner', and required one hand to assist passage of the belt into the gun. In consequence, while the hull gunner could traverse by using the pistol grip of his weapon, elevation and depression were extremely difficult. The problem was resolved by the novel method of the hull gunner inserting his head into a moulded rubber cap which was linked to the butt of the machine gun by a bar; he could then lower his head to obtain elevation, and raise it for depression.

Some mention has already been made of the smoke-bomb rack, which was prominent on the rear of Ausf. F, G and H. On later models, pending the introduction of turret dischargers, this device was concealed beneath the engine air-outlet cowling. The rack carried five bombs, held in position by spring-loaded catches. The vehicle commander released the bombs singly by a wire control which operated a ratchet wheel coupled to a camshaft. Each pull of the wire rotated the camshaft one-fifth of a turn, releasing a bomb, the pin of which was drawn by a fixed chain, and the ratchet was returned by a second spring. Thus, five pulls on the control wire would release all the bombs in succession, enabling the tank to reverse out of sight into its own smoke screen.

The design of the commander's cupola incorporated armoured shutters which could be latched in the open, intermediate or closed positions to protect the safety-glass vision blocks. Some commanders had a clock code painted round the inside of their cupolas to remind them of the turret's position in relation to the hull, a thing sometimes forgotten in the heat of action.

In normal circumstances the driver employed a direct-vision safety-glass block. In action this could be covered by a latched slab, its place being taken by a pair of periscopic binoculars, the two ports for which were visible directly above the visor. The German safety glass of the period had a slightly greenish tinge.

ORGANISATION AND TACTICS

The principal component of the Panzer division was, of course, its tank element. The establishment envisaged for the original Panzer divisions contained two two-battalion regiments, each battalion consisting of four 32-tank companies. Together with armoured command vehicles, this gave the Panzer division a total tank strength of 561 – a dream which never approached realisation.

Despite the re-armament programme, German tank production in the immediate pre-war years was sluggish and in September 1939 the majority of battalions possessed only five PzKpfw IIIs, sufficient to equip one platoon, a total of 20 per division. The balance of the divisional tank strength consisted of 24 PzKpfw IVs and light PzKpfw Is and IIs, supplemented in some cases by the recently acquired Czech 35Ts and 38Ts. Even so, the average number of tanks in the division was 320, so that battalions were forced to leave their fourth companies, i.e. 25 per cent of their paper strength, behind in their depots.

By May 1940 the situation had improved sufficiently for each of the divisions of Guderian's XIXth Panzer Corps to be equipped with 90 PzKpfw IIIs and 36 PzKpfw IVs, the divisional strength being fleshed out with PzKpfw Is and IIs. Other divisions had an establishment of 50 PzKpfw IIIs and 24 PzKpfw IVs, plus the lighter German models. Those divisions (6th, 7th and 8th) whose primary armament consisted of 37mm-armed Czech vehicles do not seem to have received an official allocation of PzKpfw IIIs, but Rommel's 7.Panzer-Division certainly acquired several, since he records the loss of six during the fighting at Arras on 21 May. Overall divisional strengths varied between 218 and 276 tanks, about half the theoretical establishment.

Following the startling success achieved in France, Hitler decided to double the number of Panzer divisions. This was achieved by halving the tank element, which was reduced to a single regiment of two battalions, although six regiments had a three-battalion establishment. By now the PzKpfw I and the 35T were considered obsolete, but the PzKpfw II was still employed for reconnaissance and there were sufficient PzKpfw IIIs to equip two 22-tank companies in each battalion. At the time of the invasion of Russia divisional strength varied between 150 and 200 tanks.

1942 saw a further rise in the number of Panzer divisions in spite of the losses of the previous year and the slow growth in tank production. On the Eastern Front the northern and central sectors remained relatively quiescent, and regiments possessed equipment for a single battalion only. On the active southern sector the number of tank battalions was increased to three, but in practical terms this meant a mere 170 tanks.

At this stage it was decided to increase the number of battalion companies to four, the old pre-war figure, but in the majority of cases the equipment was simply not available to implement the directive. Indeed, following the Stalingrad campaign and the withdrawal from the Caucasus, the average Panzer division possessed about 27 tanks.

During 1943 the PzKpfw III declined rapidly in importance as a battle tank, its place being taken by the improved PzKpfw IV and the PzKpfw V Panther, although the close-support Ausf. N continued to support Panzergrenadier operations.

The Panzer division was a balanced formation designed specifically for offensive use and much of its success depended upon its ability to generate extreme violence during the breakthrough phase of an offensive operation. With its tank brigade spearheading the assault, and close tactical support from the Luftwaffe, it would attack a sector of the enemy front not more than 5,000 yards wide. During its approach march the tanks might be concentrated in a *Keil* (wedge), but for the assault itself it would deploy either into two consecutive waves known as *Treffen* (clubs), or two parallel groups known as *Flügel* (wings), for both of which the quadruple organisation of tank units had been designed; each club or wing would be responsible for dealing with a specific aspect of the defence. The sheer weight and speed of the attack would generally take it through the defended zone, and then the Panzer brigade would accelerate towards its designated objectives.

Through the gap created by the tanks would pour the rest of the division: the armoured reconnaissance battalion, which would go into the lead and operate several miles ahead of the main body; the motorised rifle regiments, later called Panzergrenadiers, who would mop up any by-passed centres of resistance and hold selected areas of captured ground; the anti-tank units, which would form Pak-fronts against counter-attacks; the mechanised artillery batteries, ready to support the tanks with fire against specific strong points which were delaying their advance; the divisional service units, with their maintenance, supply and replenishment facilities; while within easy reach of their ground controller the *Stukageschwader* circled, ready to pounce down on pinpoint targets in their rôle as flying artillery.

Concentration and continual movement were the twin pillars of Panzer division tactics. Concentration, because the intention was to have more barrels in the gun line at the point of contact than the enemy; and continual movement, because once a breakthrough had been achieved the enemy commander would be unable to react quickly with effective

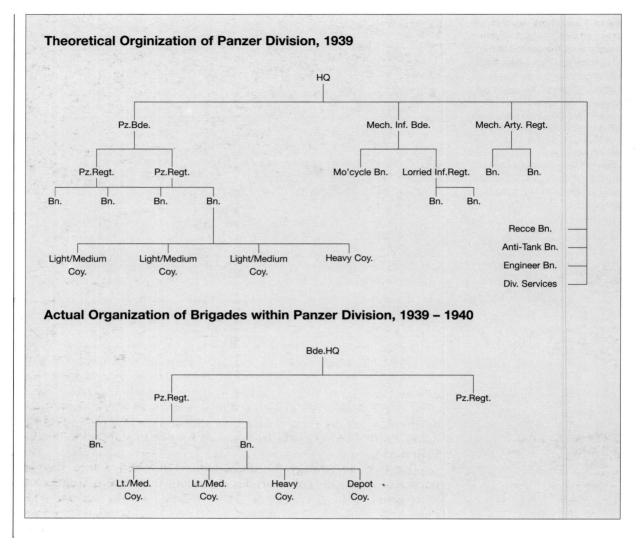

Theoretical Orginization of Panzer Division, 1939

HQ

Pz.Bde. — Pz.Regt. — Pz.Regt.
Bn. Bn. Bn. Bn.
Light/Medium Coy. — Light/Medium Coy. — Light/Medium Coy. — Heavy Coy.

Mech. Inf. Bde. — Mo'cycle Bn. — Lorried Inf.Regt.
Bn. Bn.

Mech. Arty. Regt. — Bn. — Bn.

Recce Bn.
Anti-Tank Bn.
Engineer Bn.
Div. Services

Actual Organization of Brigades within Panzer Division, 1939 – 1940

Bde.HQ

Pz.Regt. — Pz.Regt.

Bn. — Bn.
Lt./Med. Coy. — Lt./Med. Coy. — Heavy Coy. — Depot Coy.

counter-measures against a mobile force whose location remained uncertain.

If a heavily defended zone was reached it was by-passed, encircled and left for the follow-up troops, i.e. the infantry divisions, while the advance continued. In the event of an armoured counter-attack the Panzers would fight together, the burden of the engagement falling on the PzKpfw IIIs and, during the early years the, smaller PzKpfw 35Ts and PzKpfw 38Ts. If the engagement began to go against them they would adopt defensive/offensive tactics, retiring behind their own anti-tank gun screen, returning to the attack once the enemy armour had blunted its potential against this. Should it be necessary to carry out a tactical withdrawal this was undertaken by alternate bounds, the tanks working in conjunction with their anti-tank gunners.

It was, of course, the universal provision of radios which permitted this degree of flexibility, but the German Army also set much store on the personal initiative of the commanders on the spot. Command was exercised from among the division's leading elements, and more reliance was placed upon spoken as opposed to written orders than in

other armies. In addition, German commanders were adept in the rapid formation of *ad hoc* battlegroups for special operations, using any troops which happened to be immediately available.

Even after Germany had been thrown onto the strategic defensive, these principles were still employed on the Eastern Front in deep counter-attacks against an advancing enemy's flanks or rear; by then, however, the PzKpfw III was present in fewer and fewer numbers.

PZKPFW III IN ACTION

Poland

For the Polish campaign, which began on 1 September 1939, only 98 PzKpfw IIIs Ausf. A-E were available, the main burden of the fighting falling on the 1,445 PzKpfw Is and 1,223 PzKpfw IIs, supported by 211 PzKpfw IVs.

The German strategy for the campaign involved a twin double encirclement of the Polish armies defending the western frontier of their country, the first pincers being designed to close around the forward armies in their defences while the second penetrated deep into the hinterland to isolate the reserve armies which were forming. In this design the planners were materially assisted by geography, East Prussia already lying along the Poles' northern flank while the German occupation of Czechoslovakia had given them a similar advantage in the south.

Against the seven Panzer and four light armoured divisions available to the Wehrmacht, the Polish Army could oppose only 190 tanks, the majority based on the Vickers 6-ton design, and 470 more or less useless machine gun-armed tankettes; most of these vehicles were distributed among the infantry and cavalry divisions, where they could play only a subordinate role. In such circumstances defeat was inevitable, but what unhinged the Polish command system with such rapidity was the deep penetration rôle of the German armour, which in all fairness could not have been predicted.

Once through the defended zone the Panzer divisions, aided by heavy tactical air support, inflicted casualties and caused grave confusion, completing their encirclements entirely according to plan. By the time Russia intervened the Polish Army had ceased to exist as an organised entity

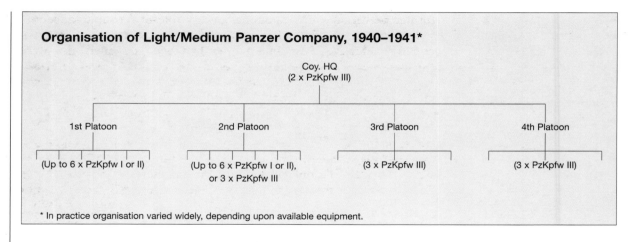

Organisation of Light/Medium Panzer Company, 1940–1941*

```
                              Coy. HQ
                          (2 x PzKpfw III)
   ┌──────────────────┬──────────────────┬──────────────────┐
1st Platoon        2nd Platoon        3rd Platoon        4th Platoon

(Up to 6 x PzKpfw I or II)   (Up to 6 x PzKpfw I or II),   (3 x PzKpfw III)   (3 x PzKpfw III)
                             or 3 x PzKpfw III
```

* In practice organisation varied widely, depending upon available equipment.

It was not, however, quite the free ride the world thought it to be at the time. This was the first occasion on which the Panzer divisions were committed en masse, and there were unforeseen difficulties, both tactical and logistic, which were encountered for the first time. For example, Guderian, whose XIXth Panzer Corps had motored across the Polish Corridor into East Prussia and then swung south into the enemy's heartland, had to apply considerable 'stick' to sub-units which became shy at the thought of a continuous drive so deep into hostile territory. On 9 September 4.Panzer-Division learned the sharp lesson that tanks have only a limited rôle to play in street fighting, being ejected from Warsaw with the loss of 60 of its Panzers. Throughout, dug-in anti-tank guns caused fearful havoc among the ranks of the thinly-armoured PzKpfw Is, and perhaps the most significant pointer to emerge from the campaign was that no assault on the West could be contemplated before the numbers of PzKpfw IIIs had risen appreciably. Luckily for Germany, the British and French left her unmolested to complete her preparations.

France and the Low Countries

On 10 May 1940 German tank strength consisted of 523 PzKpfw Is, 955 PzKpfw IIs, 349 PzKpfw IIIs, 278 PzKpfw IVs, 106 35Ts and 288 38Ts, a total of 2,499 tanks. In addition, 96 PzKpfw Is had been converted as command vehicles for lower formations, while 39 Panzerbefehlswagen IIIs had been provided for senior commanders, a clear indication that the Army as a whole was going to be led from the front.

Opposing them were 3,285 first-line French tanks of various designs, manned by an army which contemporary world opinion considered to be the true experts in armoured warfare. However, over one-third of these vehicles were distributed along the front in direct support of infantry and horsed cavalry divisions, rather like beads on a string, and could be excluded from any plan involving concerted reaction *en masse*. The French did in fact possess a number of armoured formations, of which the most experienced were the three *Divisions Légères Méchaniques* (DLM) composed of mechanised cavalry regiments, and the lessons of the Polish campaign had led to the hasty formation of four armoured divisions known as *Divisions Cuirassées* (DCR), which had barely settled down as integrated formations. The functions of the DLMs and DCRs each covered certain aspects of the Panzer divisions' potential, the former performing the traditional cavalry rôle of reconnaissance and advanced screen, while the latter's primary task was breaching the enemy's defensive crust; but neither had been designed, nor were mentally prepared for continuous fast-moving operations in the German manner. Their principal armament consisted respectively of the Somua medium tank with its 47mm gun, 56mm armour and top speed of 25mph, and the Char B heavy tank with a 37mm gun in the turret, a 75mm in the hull, 60mm armour and a speed of 17.5mph, both backed by Hotchkiss H35 light tanks, which were armed with a 37mm gun and carried 34mm armour.

At the time, the only armoured formation serving with the British Expeditionary Force was 1st Army Tank Brigade, equipped with 74 Mark I and II Matilda Infantry tanks, protected by 60mm and 78mm armour, the latter being armed with a 2pdr. gun which was marginally superior to the German 37mm. The remainder of the British armour consisted of the thin-skinned light tanks of the infantry's divisional cavalry regiments.

Thus, save in the area of light tanks, the Germans were out-numbered, out-gunned and under-armoured, and it was clear from the outset that in the inevitable tank-versus-tank fighting the burden would fall heavily on the 37mm-armed vehicles, and specifically on the PzKpfw IIIs, which carried slightly heavier armour than the Czech tanks.

On the other hand the apparent technical superiority of the French tanks was more than offset by the adoption of a one-man turret system. This meant that the vehicle commander was something of a one-man band, directing his driver, selecting ground on which to fight, loading, laying and firing the main armament and, if an officer, trying to control the other vehicles under his command as well. Few men can cope successfully with such uncompromising and simultaneous pressures, which presented a marked contrast to the smoothly efficient drill being executed in the turrets of the PzKpfw IIIs, and in consequence the standard of French tactical performance was well below that of the Germans.

Another view of the desert strewn with brewed-up armour during the 'Crusader' battles: the PzKpfw III on the left bears the 15.Panzer-Division sign in red and the DAK palm in white to the right of the driver's visor. (Martin Windrow)

The course of the 1940 campaign in France is too well known to require repetition here in detail. Briefly, the Allies expected the German Army to repeat the Schlieffen Plan, which had almost succeeded in 1914, and anticipated a 'right hook' through the Low Countries to unhinge their left, the last phase of the plan seeing them swept back against the Maginot Line in a gigantic encirclement. Such a scheme had been in the collective mind of OKW, but was replaced by a more imaginative concept based on the first of Ludendorff's 1918 *Kaiserschlacht* offensives, aimed at Amiens and the Somme estuary, the possession of which would have the effect of completely isolating the Allied armies in the north from those in the south. The thrust would be directed through the Ardennes, which were not covered by the Maginot defences since the French believed, wrongly, that the thickly wooded hills were tank-proof. The plan was conceived by Von Manstein, considered to be the Army's best operational brain, and given the name *Sichelschnitt* (Sickle Cut). In the meantime, it would do no harm to permit the Allies to believe that the old Schlieffen strategy was to be implemented, since it would draw away their reserves from the break-in sector and actually increase the number of troops caught in the trap, and for that reason an invasion of Holland and Belgium became a necessity.

When the offensive opened on 10 May the Allies reacted exactly as OKW had hoped, 1st and 7th French Armies and the BEF racing north to assist the hard-pressed Dutch and Belgians. Three days later the 3rd DLM, possibly the most effective of the French armoured formations, was acting as an advance screen while 1st Army moved into pre-determined defensive positions, and fought a hard encounter battle with 4.Panzer- Division in the Gembloux Gap.

The Germans were aided by their dive-bombers, which further distracted the already harassed French vehicle commanders, and were able to concentrate their tanks against the more dispersed enemy sub-units; but nevertheless their attack was held. The battle raged throughout the day, each side losing about 100 tanks, but many of the German vehicles were recovered when the French withdrew during the evening (The possession of or freedom to manoeuvre on a battlefield littered with abandoned tanks at the end of the day was to be a factor of great importance throughout the war a factor initially appreciated by the Germans more readily than the Allies.).

Ironically, both sides achieved their objects. 3rd DLM ensured that 1st Army settled into its positions unmolested, and the weight of 4.Panzer-Division's attack had convinced the French High Command that the major German thrust was, after all, being directed through the Low Countries.

The potentially powerful 1st and 2nd DCRs had been ordered to move north to Charleroi to counter this when Panzergruppe von Kleist, organised in two corps with a total of five Panzer divisions, burst out of the Ardennes, and the real German intentions became apparent. The two French formations were immediately ordered south to deal with the threat.

There is an ancient military maxim that the only product of order followed by counter-order is disorder, and never was the truth of this more cruelly demonstrated than on this occasion. The major French counter-attack force achieved the almost impossible feat of travelling in

1. PzKpfw III Ausf. A,
   2.Panzer-Division,
   Poland, 1939

2. PzKpfw III Ausf. E,
   2.Panzer-Division,
   Balkans, 1941

3. PzKpfw III Ausf. J,
   14.Panzer-Division,
   Russia, 1941

A

1. PzKpfw III Ausf. G, DAK, Libya, 1941

2. PzKpfw III Ausf. J,
   ex–21.Panzer-Division,
   North Africa, 1942

3. PzKpfw III Ausf. N,
   15.Panzer-Division,
   Tunisia, 1942-3

B

1. PzKpfw III Ausf. H, 10.Panzer-Division, Russia, 1941-2

2. PzKpfw III Ausf. J, 24.Panzer-Division, Russia, 1942

PANZERKAMPFWAGEN III AUSF. J

KEY

1. Front lower armour plate 50mm
2. Spare track links
3. Steering brake inspection hatch
4. 20mm Glacis plate
5. Towing bracket
6. Front upper 50mm armour plate
7. 50mm Superstructure main armour plate
8. 20mm spaced armour plate
9. 7.92mm MG 34
10. Kugelblende, armoured ball mount
11. Radio rack (Rear side)
12. 5cm KwK L/42 main gun
13. Turret ball race bullet splash guard
14. Armoured sleeve for supporting gun during recoil
15. Armoured covers for recoil brake and recuperator
16. Muzzle of 7.92mm MG 34 co-axial machine gun
17. 20mm spaced armour on 50mm gun mantlet
18. 57mm front armour on turret
19. 30mm side armour on turret
20. TZF 5f (2.5 x 24°) telescopic gun sight
21. Travel lock stay
22. 7.92mm MG 34 co-axial
23. Hand wheels for gun elevation and turret traverse
24. Fume extractor fan
25. Breech
26. Recoil guard
27. Rear right ammunition stowage bin
28. Commander's seat
29. Split hatch
30. Commanders cupola with vision blocks
31. Stowage bin for crew belongings
32. Motor inspection hatch and access to fuel tank
33. Antenna stowage tray
34. 2 meter rod antenna folded down
35. Maybach HL 120 V-12 300 PS petrol motor under armoured inspection hatch
36. Radiator fan inspection hatches
37. Tow cable
38. Cooling air intake
39. Cooling air exhaust (under rear cover)
40. Spare wheel
41. Pistol port
42. Adjustable idler wheel
43. Fire extinguisher
44. Bumpstop
45. Jack
46. 30mm superstructure side armour
47. 6 double road wheels, tyres 520/95
48. Crowbar (shortened to allow cutaway)
49. Toolbox
50. Rubber tyred return rollers
51. Flange for bolting superstructure to hull
52. Turret ball race
53. Side escape hatch
54. 30 mm side armour
55. Gunner's seat
56. Torsion bars (under floor)
57. Gunner's foot rest and pedal
58. Swing arm connected to transverse torsion bar spring
59. Driver's seat
60. Gasmask container
61. Shock absorber

62. Dry pin cast steel track Typ Kgs 61/400/120 (99 links centre guide tooth 400mm wide, 120mm pitch)
63. Steering levers
64. Gear shift lever
65. Notek blackout lighting system
66. ZF S.S.G. 77 gearbox
67. Drive sprocket
68. Instrument panel
69. Steering brake
70. Headlights with blackout covers
71. Brake cooling air intake
72. Final drive

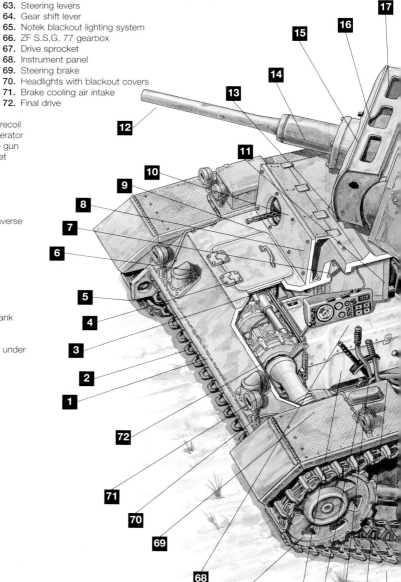

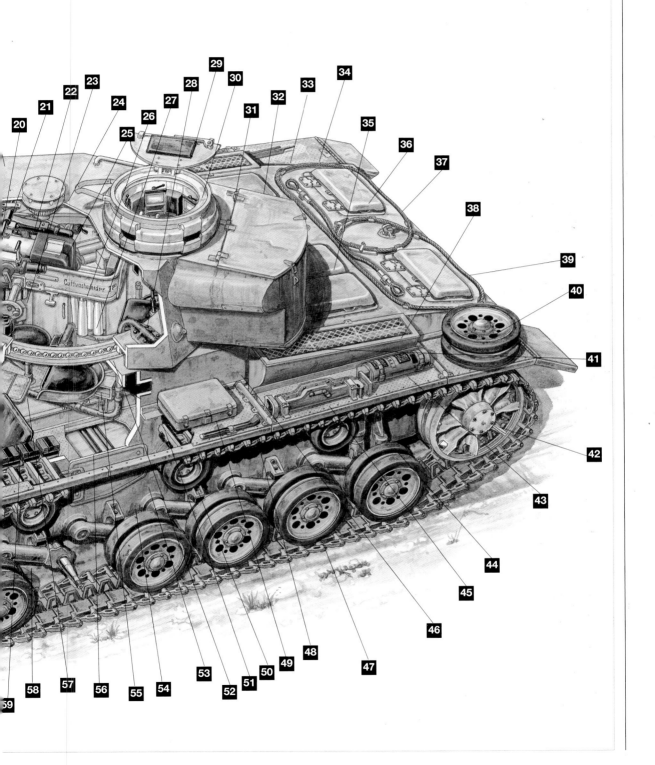

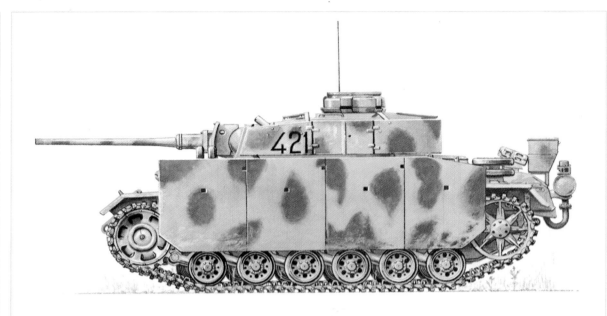

1. PzKpfw III, Ausf. M, thought to be of 3.SS-Panzer-Division 'Totenkopf', Kursk, 1943

2. PzKpfw III Ausf. J, 1.SS-Panzer-Division 'Leibstandarte Adolf Hitler', Russia, 1943

1. PzKpfw III Ausf. M, command tank, unidentified artillery unit, Russia, 1943-44

2. PzKpfw III Ausf. L, 3.SS-Panzer-Division 'Totenkopf', Kursk, July 1943

F

1. **Private, Army Panzertruppen, 1939-40**

2. **Panzer crewman, Russia, summer 1941**

3. **Panzer crewman, Deutsches Afrika Korps, 1942**

4. **Panzer crewman, 3.SS-Panzer-Division 'Totenkopf', 1942-43**

Panzerkampfwagen III Ausf. F passing through the deserted centre of a Yugoslav city, April 1941. During this campaign the terrain presented more difficulties than the enemy. (US National Archives)

several directions simultaneously, its fighting elements in some instances separated from their vital supply echelons by the width of a river. Long before they could come to grips with Von Kleist, they were bundled aside by Hoth's XVth Panzer Corps (5. and 7.Panzer-Divisions) in a series of running fights which did nothing to slow the speed of the German advance. The formidable Char Bs found themselves committed to action almost by accident, in small groups which were desperately short of fuel and without any coherent operational control. At first their appearance was unnerving, for their guns could knock out every tank in the German armoury while their stout frontal armour withstood the return 37mm fire with ease. However, after the initial shock had been overcome, German tactical expertise ensured that superior firepower, both ground and aerial, was mustered against each of the French vehicles, while tank gunners began to pick their shots with care; a shattered track would deprive a Char B of lateral as well as forward movement, so inhibiting the use of its 75mm hull-mounted gun, while a flank shot through the prominent radiator louvres would destroy the vehicle. In addition, numbers of Char Bs, their fuel tanks dry, were abandoned and set on fire by their crews to prevent capture. By the end of this sequence of encounters 1st and 2nd DCRs had ceased to count.

German armoured columns were now cutting a 30-mile swathe across France. On 15 May the 3rd DCR attempted to counter-attack the flank of this corridor south of Sedan, but was hindered by ambivalent orders, stalled, and was finally destroyed in detail. The following day the 4th

DCR, commanded by Charles de Gaulle, attacked farther west at Monteornet, and although it was successfully contained by 10. Panzer-Division, it none the less made sufficient impression to raise serious doubts in the minds of OKH and OKW.

The fact was that the Germans had not escaped these encounters uninjured; furthermore the continuous running was beginning to take its toll in the form of breakdowns, and the number of PzKpfw IIIs, upon which the Army relied for its cutting edge, was dwindling. Again, to many senior officers it seemed as though the Panzer divisions were driving straight into a trap which would clang shut as the bulk of the French armour closed in across their rear. This view overestimated not only the capability of the French armoured force, still playing a subordinate, supportive rôle many miles behind the real battlefront, but also the capacity of the enemy High Command for rapid response. However, these views could not be ignored and the doubts they raised led to heated exchanges between thrusting commanders like Guderian and his more conservative superiors. After serious consideration the advance was allowed to continue, and on 19 May Amiens was captured and the Allied armies were cut in two.

Two days later it seemed to worried officers at OKW that the anticipated thunderbolt had fallen. Near Arras the British 1st Army Tank Brigade launched a counter-attack which sliced 7.Panzer-Division in half and put the SS.Division 'Totenkopf' to flight. By evening the situation had been restored with the assistance of the Luftwaffe, but Rommel's immediate report maintained that he had been attacked by 'hundreds' of tanks, a wild exaggeration which led to the halting of the Panzer drive against the Channel Ports and even the despatch of several formations back along their own tracks to deal with the crisis.

By the time it was resumed, the Allies had recovered their balance sufficiently to organise the Dunkirk evacuation, throughout which the German armour was mistakenly held back while the Luftwaffe, at Göring's jealous request, attempted and failed to deliver the *coup de grâce.*

After a short period of rest and reorganisation the Wehrmacht turned its attention to those Allied forces which had formed a new front south of the original Panzer corridor. Such French armoured formations as still existed were in no condition to resist for long, and although the British 1st Armoured Division had landed at Cherbourg it had been scrambled together so hastily that guns, sights, ammunition and radios were all in short supply; it was, as its commander put it, a travesty of an armoured division, whose true potential was reflected by the plywood superstructure of its 'armoured' command vehicle.

The French relied on defence in depth with numerous carefully sited artillery killing grounds. These took their toll until the guns were silenced by the Luftwaffe, and then the Panzer divisions streamed south through the gaps in the broken front with nothing to stop them. The 1st Armoured Division fought a number of delaying actions but was outflanked and forced to withdraw to Cherbourg, whence it was evacuated. On 22 June France concluded an armistice with Germany.

The campaign had been won by brilliant teamwork between the Luftwaffe and the spearheads of the Panzer divisions, aided by French demoralisation and obsolete tactical doctrines. At a cost of only 156,000

Interesting view of an abandoned German field workshop in Tunisia, spring 1943. (Martin Windrow)

German casualties, of whom 60,000 were killed, Holland, Belgium and France had been conquered and the British Army forced to leave the mainland of Europe, abandoning its heavy equipment. Allied casualties totalled 2,300,000, and the huge French armoured force was all but eliminated.

But for the Panzer divisions which had done most of the fighting, the victory had not been cheap – in fact it had cost them almost half their tanks, mainly of the lighter type, from various causes. Another point which was obscured in the general euphoria was that the divisional workshop facilities had been under increasing strain towards the end, a problem that was deceptively eased by back-loading the worst breakdowns and battle casualties to Germany; in a larger context, this absence of heavy repair facilities would have most serious consequences.

For the designers of the PzKpfw III the campaign in the West represented their greatest triumph, and entirely vindicated the German concept of a main battle tank. True, the Char Bs and the Somuas had provided some anxious moments (the British Matildas had barely been encountered in the tank-versus-tank context), and for this reason the vehicle was up-gunned with a 50mm main armament, as we have already seen.

NORTH AFRICA

That the German Army was present at all in this improbable theatre was due to the shattering defeat inflicted on the Italians by Wavell's 'Thirty Thousand' during late 1940 and early 1941. Sent by Hitler to bolster his shaky ally with strictly limited resources and an equally limited brief, Generalleutnant Erwin Rommel, former commander of 7.Panzer- Division, discovered a weakness in the British dispositions at Mersa Brega and, contrary to his orders, attacked on 3 March 1941. The attack broke through the flimsy defensive screen and the ruthless exploitation that followed compelled the evacuation not only of the Benghazi bulge but of the whole of Cyrenaica, with the exception of the port of Tobruk. By 13 April the Axis forces were on the Egyptian frontier and had taken the strategically important Halfaya Pass.

On 19 April an attempt was made to penetrate the Tobruk perimeter. The Australian infantry let the leading PzKpfw IIIs pass over them and then engaged the follow-up troops, who were compelled to go to ground. The German tanks were then subjected to fire from the hull-down Cruisers of 'B' and 'C' Squadrons 1st Royal Tank Regt. and the Matildas of 'D' Squadron, 7 RTR; they lost several vehicles and were bundled back the way they had come.

At dawn on the morning of 15 May Halfaya Pass fell to a *coup de main* carried out by 'C' Squadron, 4 RTR, another Matilda regiment. Rommel was adamant that the Pass should be retaken, and on 27 May no less than 160 tanks, organised in three battlegroups and led by PzKpfw IIIs, converged towards its head. An incredible sight met the eyes of their commanders; nine Matildas, all that 'C' Squadron could muster, were crawling out to meet them, covering the withdrawal of their infantry down onto the coastal plain.

Eagerly the German gunners set their sights and loosed off round after round, only to see the 37mm and 50mm shot go flying off the Matildas' thick hides. Unlike the Char B, the Matilda did not have vulnerable radiator louvres, and its tracks were better protected; in addition, the drill in its three-man turret was every bit as efficient as that in the PzKpfw III, and the return fire of the 2pdrs. could penetrate the armour of every German and Italian vehicle present at the normal battle range of 500 to 800 yards. German tanks in the leading ranks of the *Kiel* began to explode and burn with out any apparent reduction in the enemy's strength. Those behind, even less capable of engaging on even terms, started a retrogressive movement which soon took an entire battalion out of range. Satisfied, the three surviving Matildas retired

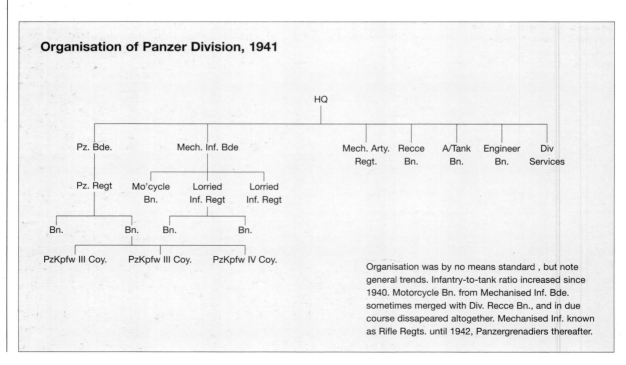

Organisation of Panzer Division, 1941

Organisation was by no means standard , but note general trends. Infantry-to-tank ratio increased since 1940. Motorcycle Bn. from Mechanised Inf. Bde. sometimes merged with Div. Recce Bn., and in due course dissapeared altogether. Mechanised Inf. known as Rifle Regts. until 1942, Panzergrenadiers thereafter.

The PzKpfw III's most famous derivative, the *Sturmgeschütz* (assault gun). This early example, armed with a L/24 75mm howitzer, was one of only four batteries employed during the 1940 campaign in France. (RAC Tank Museum)

down the Pass, picking up the crews of the six which had been immobilised by track damage.

Such an event was unparalleled in the history of the Panzerwaffe, and Rommel was beside himself with rage at the propaganda victory handed to the British. The unfortunate battalion commander was court-martialled, his immediate superior dismissed out of hand, and the commander of 5.Light-Division removed from his post. That there existed among Panzer crews a very real fear of the Matilda was quite understandable, for the only effective defence at the time was the 88mm anti-aircraft gun firing in the anti-tank role. However, '88s' were only to be had at a premium, and an immediate request was made for Panzerjäger to be despatched to Africa to restore the balance.

In June the British mounted their first major offensive to relieve Tobruk, Operation 'Battleaxe', capturing Fort Capuzzo on the 15th. At first light the following day 15.Panzer-Division launched a counter-attack, but drove into an ambush laid by 'A' and 'B' Squadrons, 7 RTR. Fifty of the division's 80 fighting vehicles were lost before it was able to extricate itself. The divisional commander, mindful of the fate of his colleagues following the Halfaya débâcle, quickly regrouped and by-passed Capuzzo, hoping to isolate it from the east; his only reward was to be stalled yet again by Matildas, this time manned by 'B' Squadron, 4 RTR, at a ridge known as Point 206.

Farther south, 5.Light-Division was fighting a successful offensive/defensive battle against the Cruisers of 7th Armoured Brigade whose two regiments (2 and 6 RTR) had blunted their potential against an anti-tank

gun screen at Hafid Ridge. 5th Light's Panzers had then sallied forth to engage the 'Desert Rats' in a running fight during which 6 RTR's new Crusader tanks broke down at an alarming rate. The German intention was to sweep north to the coast, thus trapping the British troops in the Capuzzo area; but before this could be achieved 'Battleaxe' was cancelled and an escape corridor held open by two Matilda squadrons, each of which held off an entire German division for a day.

During the tank battles the British had knocked out more than 100 German tanks, but only 12 of these were completely written off, the rest being recovered and repaired. Their own loss had been 91 vehicles, many of them simple breakdowns which could have been recovered had it not been for high-level muddle and misunderstanding. This time it was the heads of senior British officers which rolled.

It was not until November that a further attempt was made to relieve Tobruk. Operation 'Crusader' was a much larger affair than 'Battleaxe' and included three armoured brigades (4th, 7th and 22nd) as well as two tank brigades, the 1st covering the northern flank with XIII Corps, and the 32nd the Tobruk garrison's break-out. British first line tank strength was 756, that of the Axis 320.

But while Rommel fought with both his Panzer divisions concentrated (5.Light had been restyled as 21.Panzer), the British armoured brigades each pursued their separate objectives, with the result that within days of the start of the offensive 7th Armoured Brigade was removed from the board while the 4th and 22nd were left confused and dispersed. However, Rommel's brief foray into Egypt by which he hoped, unsuccessfully, to destroy the British commander's nerve, provided just sufficient time for a reorganisation to be carried out. Tobruk was relieved by XIII Corps, isolated again, and finally relieved for the last time while sheer attrition, both tactical and mechanical, reduced the German strength to such a dangerous level that Cyrenaica had to be evacuated. Some 300 Axis tanks had been destroyed as opposed to a British loss of 187. In addition to the casualties sustained by the Panzer divisions in actions with the British armour, other causes of loss included breakdowns induced by the PzKpfw III's inefficient air filters, and tanks destroyed by 2pdr. *portees* and 25pdrs. firing over open sights, a reminder that the British did not hold a monopoly in charging unshaken gunlines.

Rommel's remarkable resilience was demonstrated in January 1942 when, having received a meagre reinforcement of tanks, he riposted so unexpectedly that much of the lost ground was recovered, the line eventually being stabilised at Gazala. Here both sides began to build up their strength for the next round. *Panzerarmee Afrika* eventually accumulated 228 Italian tanks, 50 PzKpfw IIs, 40 75mm howitzer PzKpfw IVs, 223 L/42 50mm PzKpfw IIIs and 19 L/60 50mm PzKpfw IIIs, a total of 560 tanks. Opposing them would be 843 British tanks, of which the most significant were the 167 Grants, new arrivals in the desert, which, with their sponson-mounted 75mm guns put the British ahead for once in tank-killing potential.

The Axis got in the first and vital blow on 27 May. The Grants tore great holes in the ranks of the Panzer divisions; but the British fought in the same uncoordinated fashion they had employed during 'Crusader', missed price-less opportunities, and ultimately suffered a disastrous defeat which cost them most of their armour and which was followed almost immediately by the surrender of Tobruk. It was the PzKpfw IIIs crowning achievement in Africa, and earned Rommel his Field Marshal's baton.

The *Afika Korps* had also suffered severely, and the pursuit of the beaten 8th Army was carried out with a mere handful of tanks. These succeeded in turning the British out of their defensive position at Mersa Matruh, but lacked the necessary 'clout' to penetrate the newly forming line at El Alamein.

By the end of August Rommel had been reinforced sufficiently to attempt a repeat of the right hook with which he had begun the Gazala/Knightsbridge battle. In addition to 243 Italian M13s, he had 71 L/60 and 93 L/42 PzKpfw IIIs, 10 of the older PzKpfw IVs and a handful of light tanks; of greater significance was the arrival of 27 PzKpfw IVF2s, armed with an L/43 75mm gun, which would become his cutting edge – a clear indication that the PzKpfw III was now falling below battlefield

Nice study of PzKpfw III Ausf. Js of 24.Panzer-Division moving into a forward zone during the 1942 Russian campaign. This formation favoured large rear stowage boxes, on which were marked the divisional sign, commemorating its origins in the old 1.Kavallerie-Division – see Plate C. 24.Panzer-Division was lost at Stalingrad, but reformed several months later. (Bundesarchiv)

requirements. In the event, the offensive was severely checked at Alam Halfa ridge and the Axis army thrown onto the defensive by an acute shortage of fuel.

This was a factor which the 8th Army's new commander, Lt.-Gen. Bernard Montgomery, intended to exploit to the full in the planning for the Second Battle of Alamein. 8th Army would fight a 'crumbling' battle, attacking first in one place and then another, forcing the Panzer divisions to burn irreplaceable petrol driving between sectors in the counter-attack rôle. It was a strategy against which Rommel had no effective defence, since a breakthrough would spell annihilation for his army.

Later models of the StuG were armed with a high-velocity gun; this type of mantlet was known as a *Saukopf* (pig's head). The vehicle has also been fitted with side skirts as a defence against hollow-charge weapons such as that held by the infantryman in the foreground. (Bundesarchiv)

When the battle began on 23 October 8th Army could deploy over 1,000 tanks, including 170 Grants and 252 Shermans, with more in reserve. Axis tank strength was 278 MI3s, 85 L/42 and 88 L/60 PzKpfw IIIs, eight old PzKpfw IVs and 30 PzKpfw IVF2s. During major tank engagements such as Tel el Aqqaqir the British lost the greater number of vehicles, but Rommel's strength was effectively whittled away until defeat became inevitable. By the time the battle ended the Italian armoured divisions had ceased to exist and all but a handful of German tanks had been destroyed or abandoned on the battlefield, while the *Afrika Korps* began its long withdrawal to Tunisia.

Most of the subsequent fighting took place in mountainous country. With the Anglo-American 1st Army closing in on their last African bridgehead the Germans hastily shipped over 10.Panzer-Division, sufficient tanks to re-equip 15. and 21.Panzer-Divisions, and a Tiger battalion. A notable success was gained against the US 1st Armoured Division at Kasserine Pass, but the end could not be long delayed, and on 12 May 1943 the war in Africa was officially over. (See New Vanguard 4, *Churchill Infantry Tank, 1941-51*)

During the final phase the PzKpfw III remained the most numerous tank in the German order of battle, but an increasing number of those reaching the front were the 75mm-armed Ausf. N. 'The reasons why the 75mm short gun was gaining favour at the expense of the long 50mm gun seem to have been mainly two. The nature of the fighting tipped the balance towards HE rather than armour-piercing shell, while the introduction of hollow-charge ammunition for the 75mm gun in the summer of 1942 improved its all-round usefulness.'*

The Balkans

Hitler had long sought a confrontation with Bolshevik Russia, and his offensive would have been launched in the spring of 1941 had he not been forced to secure his right flank by invading Yugoslavia and rescuing Mussolini's armies from their hopeless involvement with the Greeks. These short campaigns had demonstrated once again the decisive teamwork between the Luftwaffe and the Panzer divisions, and were notable for the determination of the German tank crews to force their

---

*The British official history of the campaign, The Mediterranean and Middle East, Vol. IV, page 500, Major General I.S.O. Playfair and others.

machines through some of the most difficult country in Europe; they also absorbed valuable time which would have to be subtracted from the operational period available before the onset of the Russian winter.

The poorly equipped Yugoslav army, riven as it was by racial, religious and political differences, was not a formidable opponent and, moreover, it adopted the flawed strategy of defending its frontiers, just as the French and the Poles had done. Using their well-tried formula, the Panzer divisions quickly effected penetrations and advanced along the principal valleys, leaving the Yugoslav's cordon defences isolated. The interest in their operations lies in the staggered timing of their assaults around the long frontier, the intention being to keep the enemy in a state of uncertain ferment with every fresh penetration, and in the way that the country was quickly carved into sections by converging attacks on the main cities executed by different formations. There was very little fighting, one senior German officer describing the Panzer divisions' progress as being akin to a military parade. Hostilities had begun on 6 April 1941; when Yugoslavia surrendered unconditionally eleven days later no less than 345,000 of her soldiers marched into captivity. Total German casualties from all causes amounted to a mere 558.

Greece did not prove to be such a walk-over, although the nature of the Greek Army's deployment made an Axis victory a virtual certainty, for of the 21 Greek divisions available, no less than 15 were already engaged with the Italians in Albania, while the left flank of the defence lines fronting Bulgaria were wide open to attack from Yugoslavia.

In places the Panzer divisions encountered the toughest possible resistance, but the thrust through the Greek centre proved decisive. When the Greeks surrendered on 23 April a recently arrived British corps fell back to the famous Pass of Thermopylae. There, the following day, 19 tanks of I/Panzer Regiment 31, 5.Panzer Division, unwisely tried to batter their way through the defile in single file. This was not the sort of liberty to take with experienced troops and every one was either knocked out or set ablaze. The British continued their withdrawal to Kalamata in the Peloponnese, where, by 28 April, most of them were evacuated by sea, having been forced to abandon all their heavy equipment. During the campaign over 70,000 Greeks were killed or wounded and 270,000 captured, while the British sustained nearly 12,000 casualties; German losses came to 4,500 personnel plus an unacceptable number of tanks. Unseen damage consisted of lost time and cumulative wear and tear on the Panzer divisions' vehicles, both of which would have a baleful effect on the conduct of operations in the Soviet Union.

Russia

No one really knows how many tanks the Soviet Union possessed in 1941, but the lowest estimate places the figure at not less than 20,000. They varied from multi-turreted dinosaurs like the T-100, T-35 and T-28 to the small amphibious T-37 tankettes. By Western standards they were crudely finished, but they were robust and intentionally

An interesting late model *Panzerbefehlswagen III* (command vehicle) immobilised by mine damage to its left track on a primitive Russian road. The co-axial machine gun has been replaced by an armoured observation visor, to the left of which can be seen a battery of three smoke grenade dischargers. Two further vision ports can be seen in the hull, just below the turret. The normally prominent frame radio antenna has been folded flat. (Charles K. Kliment)

simple in layout, since their crews were drawn from an as-yet tecnically unsophisticated population.

For many years the Russians had followed the French theory of infantry support, leading the attack with heavy tanks and following up with T-26s accompanying the foot-soldiers, while exploitation formations equipped with the fast BT Series stood by ready to exploit the breakthrough. However, the success of the German *blitzkrieg* tactics in Poland and France, together with their own shortcomings in Spain and Finland, had led Red Army commanders to appreciate the flaws in their doctrine and to design formations which bore some resemblance to the Panzer divisions. It was unfortunate that the basic structure of the Soviet armoured corps was in this transitional stage when Hitler launched his invasion.

This was bad enough, but in addition Russian tactical response was infinitely slower even than the French. A totalitarian, ruthlessly centralised state required absolute obedience rather than initiative from all but its most senior officers and since the officer corps had been mercilessly purged of progressive elements during the 1930s the safest course for an individual was to wait for orders from above. This was hardly an ideal situation in which to enter a battle the tempo of which would be dictated by Panzer commanders who made their decisions among their leading vehicles and whose goal was continuous mobility. To compound a thoroughly unsatisfactory state of affairs, Russian armoured units lacked tactical flexibility since the issue of radios extended downwards only as far as battalion commanders, so that orders on the move could only be transmitted between vehicles by flag or hand signal.

On the other hand, the Russians had some brilliant designers who were particularly skilled in producing vehicles with a sound gun/armour relationship. The new KV heavy and the T-34 medium tanks both carried a 76.2mm gun which was better than anything the Panzerwaffe possessed, while the KV's armour was comparable to the British Matilda's; the T-34's angled plate was almost as good, and its Christie suspension gave running speeds well in excess of those of the German battle tanks (see New Vanguard 20, *T-34/85 Medium Tank 1944-94*).

The onslaught on Russia, Operation 'Barbarossa', began on 22 June 1941. Germany had available 3,200 tanks, of which 1,440 were PzKpfw IIIs and 517 PzKpfw IVs; a total of 17 armoured divisions, organised in four Panzergruppen, took part in the initial assault. The forward units of the Red Air Force were destroyed on the ground and the tank spearheads began to roll forward. When encountered, resistance was fierce but uncoordinated. German operators monitoring the radio frequencies of higher Russian formations heard time and again the plaintive request, 'What are we to do? We must have orders!' But few men had the courage to make decisions without consulting higher authority, and those who did found that by the time their orders reached the troops, the tactical situation was radically different from that in which they had been conceived. Repeatedly the Panzergruppen wheeled together to form huge pockets which were reduced by the follow-up infantry divisions, yielding vast numbers of prisoners and enormous quantities of equipment. In Moscow, Stalin reacted in characteristic Soviet fashion by demanding a scapegoat, and shot his leading tank

An unidentified PzKpfw III battalion passes a ruined village in the Mius-Stalino area, August 1943. The lead vehicle has a turret-girdle of spaced armour but appears to carry side-skirts on the far side only. (Bundesarchiv)

expert a step which failed to bring about any radical improvement in the Red Army's position.

It was a staggering débâcle, which ultimately cost the Red Army 1,000,000 men, and 17,000 tanks knocked out, captured or simply abandoned by their crews after they had broken down. In a little over three weeks one Panzer group alone advanced 400 miles; and it seemed as though Moscow, hub of the all-important Russian railway system, was there for the taking.

But other factors were also at work. In France the Panzer divisions had been set an objective that was mechanically attainable, the Channel; in Russia the objectives were so far distant that the German heavy repair system simply could not cope with the numbers of breakdowns, which increased with every mile covered. Again, battle casualties had been higher than in previous campaigns, accounting for 2,700 vehicles, so that after ten weeks' fighting the Panzer spearheads had been reduced to mere shadows of their former selves.

Whether Moscow could have been taken before the deteriorating weather brought all movement to a standstill remains an open question, but Hitler's meddling with the dispositions of the Panzergruppen certainly provided the Red Army with an unexpected bonus in time. Russia survived, and her limitless potential would ensure that the scales would tilt slowly but irrevocably against Nazi Germany.

When tank had met tank, the PzKpfw IIIs had dealt easily with the elderly T-35s, the T-26s and the thin-skinned BTs; but the KV provided an unpleasant surprise. Squatting on a causeway, a single KV could hold up an entire Panzer division for a day, shrugging off rounds from every gun that could be brought to bear, and in such circumstances the only effective answer was for German infantry to stalk the brute with explosive charges. The 37mm gun was useless against these monsters, and although the L/42 50mm could score a kill this was usually achieved at a range of 50 yards or less, and preferably from the rear. The superb T-34 was an even greater headache for Panzer crews who sincerely believed at the start of the campaign that they held a wide lead in technology over their Russian counterparts, and as far as the PzKpfw III was concerned not even the fitting of the L/60 gun could bridge the gap; the balance was redressed, bloodily, by inept Russian tactics opposed to German expertise and initiative.

For the Wehrmacht, the major event of 1942 was the great drive into the Caucasus in pursuit of the Baku oilfields. Once more the tank columns motored across the steppe under cloudless skies, and as the miles disappeared beneath their tracks it seemed as though the Panzer divisions were to enjoy a second 'Happy Time'. There was, in fact, very little fighting, for the Red Army had learned its lesson and had sidestepped the principal thrust.

But on the eastern flank of the advance lay Stalingrad, concerning which Hitler developed a total megalomania. All available reserves were diverted to the capture of the city, a fact duly noted by the Russian Supreme Command (*Stavka*), which responded with a gigantic double envelopment, trapping the German 6th Army, and part of 4th Panzer Army as well, which had been forced against its better judgement to take part in the street-fighting. The bitter struggle continued until 2 February 1943, when the newly created Field Marshal von Paulus surrendered with 200,000 of his men.

Stalingrad had been a disaster which not only shook the German Army to its core, but which also opened the door on the even more horrendous possibility of the Red Army encircling those forces now hastily withdrawing from the Caucasus; all that was needed was a determined thrust south-west to the Sea of Azov, and their fate would be sealed.

Stavka detailed two armies for the task, Vatutin's South-West Front and Golikov's Voronezh Front, and for a while they had a free run. This was permitted as a matter of deliberate policy by Von Manstein, the Commander-in-Chief of Army Group South, who was fully aware of Soviet intentions. He appreciated that because of Russian inexperience in deep-penetration operations and poor logistic back-up, both Soviet armies would quickly outrun their supply echelons and that the inevitable breakdowns would steadily drain away the strength of their tank formations conversely, he did not wish to launch his own counter-offensive until the German armour had been sufficiently concentrated for a knock-out blow, for Stalingrad had cost the Army 800 Panzers and the average strength of his Panzer divisions was now 27 tanks.

On 20 February 1943 he moved at last, slicing into Vatutin's flank and finding most of the Russian columns stalled for want of fuel. South-West Front was routed and forced into a precipitate retreat, losing 615 tanks, 400 guns, 23,000 men killed and 9,000 captured. Golikov, hastening to his stricken comrade's aid, was caught while still deploying and handled even more severely. Voronezh Front was thrown back across the Donets, leaving behind 600 tanks, 500 guns and 40,000 casualties. Only the *rasputitsa*, the great thaw which turned hard-frozen ground into impassable mud, brought an end to Von Manstein's runaway progress.

This operation completely restored the integrity of the Eastern Front, and was the last occasion on which the PzKpfw III played the major role in a successful strategic offensive; indeed, it was the Panzerwaffe's last strategic success of the war, for in July its potential was irrevocably blunted against the interminable defensive belts of the Kursk salient, and then written down in the great tank battle of Prokhorovka, the largest of the Second World War, in which machines rammed each other or fought murderous duels at point-blank range. Kursk cost the Germans 1,500 tanks, which could not be spared, and the Russians about the same, which were replaced almost at once from factories safe beyond the Urals.

Thereafter, the PzKpfw III soldiered on in decreasing numbers, its place as the Panzer divisions' main battle tank being taken by the PzKpfw IV and the Panther, its last actions being fought during the great defensive battles of 1944.

Technically the PzKpfw III was, despite minor faults, a well-balanced basic design which left provision for up-gunning and up-armouring, but by 1942 it was incapable of further modification that would enable it to keep pace with the spiral of the gun/armour race. During the high years of *blitzkrieg* it was the only weapon in the German tank arsenal that really counted and thus, like Napoleon's *vieux moustaches*, it did not merely witness history in the making – it made it, from the Channel to the Volga

Later versions of the *Panzerbefehlswagen III* dispensed with the frame aerial and employed a branched antenna instead, as carried by this example working with a Panzergrenadier unit. (Bundesarchiv)

and from the Arctic to the North African desert. This achievement has, perhaps, been overshadowed in recent years by the study of later and more dramatic German designs, but the fact remains that it was the PzKpfw III that brought Hitler closest to achieving his wildest dreams.

The PzKpfw III

BASIC TECHNICAL DETAILS

Ausf. F

Weight:	20 tons (Ausf. M: 20.8 tons)
Crew:	5
Armament:	1 X KwK L/42 50mm gun
	(Ausf. M: 1 X KwK 39 L/60 50mm gun)
	2 X 7.92mm machine guns
Armour:	30mm (Ausf. M: 30mm plus 20mm or 30mm)
Engine:	Maybach HL 120TRM, 300hp
Speed:	25mph
Overall length:	17ft. 9in. (Ausf. M: 21ft. 6in.)
Width:	9ft. 7in. (Ausf. M: 9ft. 9in.)
Height:	8ft. 3in.

THE PLATES

A1: PZKPFW III AUSF. A, 2.PANZER-DIVISION, POLAND,1939

The overall colour scheme is standard 'Panzer grey', with the large white '223' on the turret side identifying Company, *Zug* and vehicle respectively. During this campaign Polish anti-tank gunners took a far heavier toll of the Panzers than was realised by the rest of the world, and the plain white German national cross used at first was soon considered to be far too conspicuous. A normal practice was to paint it over in yellow, sometimes – as here – leaving a thin white border. The division's first tactical sign, two yellow dots, appears over the inner side of the driver's visor. The operations of this division took them through an area cut by numerous small streams, and this crew have acquired a rough fascine of pine logs to ease their passage.

A2: PZKPFW III AUSF. E, 2.PANZER-DIVISION, BALKANS, 1941

Panzer Regiment 3, the tank component of this formation, abandoned large turret numbers and marked smaller on the forward side-plates of the hull. For internal recognition purposes coloured geometric symbols were painted on the turret sides – in the case of the 4th Company, an open red triangle on a yellow square. Another peculiarity of this company, at least, was the fixing of a polished horseshoe in a prominent position on the offside track-guard. Note the divisional sign, now one of the combinations of Y-rune and bars used by most formations, left of the driver's visor. The white stripe under it is unexplained.

A3: PZKPFW III AUSF. J, 14.PANZER-DIVISION, RUSSIA, 1941

The all-grey scheme is enlivened by the rarely seen white Panzer rhombus marking on the turret sides and rear bin, beneath the vehicle number '14'. These markings are repeated on the spare turret bin lying on the engine deck. The 'K' probably indicates a company commander's vehicle. White outline crosses of the type standard for this period appear on the hull side and rear, and an air recognition flag is draped over the turret roof. The yellow divisional sign, similar to an Odalrune, is marked on the offside of the rear hull plate.

B1: PZKPFW III AUSF. G, DAK, LIBYA, 1941

There is a definite 'early days' look about this Ausf. G; the original Panzer grey is starting to show through the hastily applied sand-yellow 'slap'. The turret carries the number '612' in red trimmed with white, and the *Afrika Korps* palm and swastika are marked small on the hull side beneath the turret door forward hinge line. A large air recognition flag is lashed over the stowage on the rear deck; and the addition of road wheels and tracks to the front armour testify to an awareness of the 'Matilda menace'. A meticulous gunner has manufactured his own canvas muzzle cover and mounting sleeve, to protect his 'baby' as far as possible from the dust. The slung sun-helmets suggest a recently arrived crew – most old hands threw these over the side, as being about the most useless headgear for a tank-man that could be conceived.

B2: PZKPFW III AUSF. J, EX-21.PANZER-DIVISION, NORTH AFRICA, 1942

The history of this pale sand-yellow Ausf. J can be read in its markings. In the centre of the front plate is 21.Panzer-Division's tactical sign in white; the turret carries the white outline numbers 'III' indicating that the original owners were 1st Company, Panzer Regiment 22. It then seems to have enjoyed a spell in British service, perhaps after abandonment due to a breakdown; for on the offside front is the rhinoceros sign of 1st Armoured Division, and on the nearside the tactical number 86, indicating 9th Lancers. That some attempt was made to take the tank into regimental service is attested by the 'B' Squadron square painted on the turret; but this attempt was undoubtedly stamped upon, and the vehicle was sent back for evaluation, acquiring the evaluation number 'A100' in the process.

B3: PZKPFW III AUSF. N, 15.PANZER-DIVISION, TUNISIA, 1942–1943

The track links draped over the turret roof of this Ausf. N. reflect the growing Allied air superiority of this period; additional track links and sandbags are also fitted to the front of the hull. As yet this tank seems to have seen little wear and tear, and the dark mustard shade favoured (along with olive green) for German armour in Tunisia is still intact. The turret numbers are '04', in black outlined with white; the national cross on the hull side is also black and white. The divisional sign is painted beside the driver's visor in the red usually employed by this division. It is interesting that this vehicle lacks the three smoke dischargers normally mounted on each turret side of this Mark – a photograph in this book shows them fitted to the next tank in this troop.

C1: PZKPFW III AUSF. H, 10.PANZER-DIVISION, RUSSIA, 1941–1942

The national cross, in white outline, is painted on a supplementary bin which has been welded to the track-guard; behind this, the vehicle serial number '621' is painted on a black rhomboid plate, a system favoured in the immediate pre-war years. The tank's precise place in the regimental order of battle is not revealed by the single number '5', in red outlined white, on the turret side; to the rear of this is the white-sprayed outline of Panzer Regiment 7's bison badge. The yellow divisional sign is visible beside the driver's side visor.

C2: PZKPFW III AUSF. J, 24.PANZER-DIVISION, RUSSIA, 1942

In common with many tanks of this division photographed in Russia, this L/60 Ausf. J has a large stowage bin fixed across the rear of the engine deck, and on this can be seen the black and white national cross and the division's distinctive sign. A log has been lashed below the bin, doubtless as an unditching beam. The turret number '525' in red, outlined white, identifies the 2nd *Zug*, 5th Company. The origins of this formation, raised from the old 1.Kavallerie-Division, are recalled in the yellow uniform piping which contrasted with the rose-coloured *Waffenfarbe* of the rest of the Army tank units.

D: CUTAWAY OF PZKPFW III AUSF. J,
See the cutaway key for details

E1:PZKPFW III AUSF. M, THOUGHT TO BE OF 3.SS-PANZER-DIVISION 'TOTENKOPF' KURSK, 1943

The new standard overall colour scheme of dark yellow, with added camouflage in the form of red-brown blotches, covers even the spare track links on the tank's nose and the large wooden stowage crate on the rear deck. The forward plate of the hull skirt armour is missing, but the turret-girdle is intact, and bears the tank number '421' in plain black.

E2: PZKPFW III AUSF. J, 1.SS-PANZER-DIVISION 'LEIBSTANDARTE ADOLF HITLER', RUSSIA, 1943

Photographed, possibly near Belgorod, towards the end of Von Manstein's 1943 offensive, this tank still wears basic Panzer grey, but has been heavily overpainted with white snow camouflage. The rear face of the turret bin has been left grey as a background to the white-outline tank number '555', which has been roughly repainted in red on the turret sides. Grey areas have also been left around the national cross on the hull side, and the divisional sign on the nearside of the rear hull plate. The national cross is repeated beside this.

Another view of a *Panzerbefehlswagen III*, taken in 1944; the markings are interesting – see Plate F and commentary. (Bundesarchiv)

F1: PZKPFW III AUSF. M COMMAND TANK, UNIDENTIFIED ARTILLERY UNIT RUSSIA 1943–1944

By this stage of the war the PzKpfw III was of little use as a main battle tank, but numbers served on as headquarters vehicles with heavy tank destroyer battalions – a position hinted at by the turret number '001'. The overall dark yellow colour scheme has been sprayed with streaks of red-brown and dark green; the forward plate of the rather hard-worn skirt armour is evidently a replacement. The tank's outline is partly broken up by the addition of birch saplings – we have 'thinned out' this foliage for clarity. The national cross on the turret girdle is unusual in that the centre is in the yellow ground-colour, inside a thin black cross outlined with white. At the front bottom corner of the girdle is the name 'Brigitte' in white Gothic script. The commander wears artillery uniform.

F2: PZKPFW III AUSF. L, 3.SS-PANZER-DIVISION 'TOTENKOPF', KURSK, JULY 1943

Note the large strap-iron stowage rack welded across the

rear hull; these were common, and as they were strictly a unit modification they took many varying forms. The tank number '823' is roughly painted on the rear of the turret bin, without white trim. On the nearside of the rear hull plate is the three-pronged temporary divisional sign adopted for the Kursk offensive, Operation *'Zitadelle'*. Another variant of the national cross appears on the offside, this one a 'Luftwaffe' style of thin proportions, black outlined with white with a black outer trim.

G1: PRIVATE, ARMY PANZERTRUPPEN, 1939–1940

The two-piece padded beret bears national insignia in white thread, and the national eagle also appears on the right breast of the double-breasted black 'crossover' tunic The shirt is 'mouse grey', the tie black. The tunic is piped round the upper lapel and collar in the rose *Waffenfarbe* of this arm of service; the patches on the collar, piped in rose and bearing white metal death's-heads, were common to all ranks of the Panzerwaffe up to and frequently including general officers. The similarly piped shoulder-straps, sewn down to prevent snagging in the vehicle, are of the plain design worn by all ranks up to Unteroffizier. He holds a round of 37mm High Explosive with a trace in the base of the projectile, this being indicated by the silver-painted head and yellow band.

G2: PANZER CREWMAN, RUSSIA, SUMMER 1941

The shoulder-straps from the black tunic are worn here on the shirt – these were the only authorised insignia for the shirt. The black Army-pattern sidecap of 1940 issue has the national eagle in less visible pale grey thread on black backing, and the national cockade is enclosed by a V of rose piping. He holds a round of Armour-Piercing Capped ammunition for the 'short' L/42 50mm gun.

G3: PANZER CREWMAN, DEUTSCHES AFRIKA KORPS, 1942

The tropical version of the sidecap, in Olive Drab lined with red cloth, was often much faded, and it was fashionable to deliberately bleach them with anti-gas capsules, so that a pale sandy shade was quite common. Insignia are embroidered on a tan ground, the national eagle being in pale blue-grey thread. The usual V of rose *Waffenfarbe* is worn. The shirt is similarly bleached, and bears the olive cloth shoulder-straps from the tropical uniform, piped rose, with an olive-painted button. The white metal identity disc bore the man's particulars on each side of the central perforations. He has evidently just cleared the turret of hot spent cases, hence the gloves; he holds an Armour-Piercing AP.40 round for the 'short' 50mm L/42.

Ausf. M with skirt armour and turret girdle, by-passing a culvert which engineers are constructing across a stream for wheeled transport. Comparison with other photographs gives a probable identification of 3. SS-Panzer-Division 'Totenkopf' on its way to take part in the Kursk 'death ride', July 1943. See Plate E. (Bundesarchiv)

G4: PANZER CREWMAN, 3.SS-PANZER-DIVISION 'TOTENKOPF', 1942–1943

The black sidecap, bearing Waffen-SS national eagle and SS death's-head badges in silver-grey thread, is of the distinctive cut used by the SS and Luftwaffe formations. It is tied on his head with a scarf against the bitter Russian winter; and he also wears the black Panzer jacket buttoned across and closed to the throat. The front join of the SS pattern was vertical, rather than slanted in the Army manner. The collar is not piped, and bears two identical silver-grey thread death's-head devices. This was peculiar to this formation, whose insignia was the death's-head; normally Waffen-SS privates wore divisional insignia on the right collar only, and a blank black patch on the left. The SS-pattern national eagle appears on the upper left sleeve, and the divisional cuff-title on the same forearm. The rose of the armoured troops appears only as piping on the shoulder-straps and in a V on the cap front. He holds a round of High Explosive ammunition for the 'long' L/60 50mm gun.